LiFE LESSoNS

from Cats!

Keepsake Gift Book

A Gift For:

_____

From:

_____

Friends come in many shapes, sizes, and colors.

Every day is a good day to learn something new.

Stop and smell the flowers—unless there's a bee on it. If there's a bee, just move on and smell something else.

Always proceed with caution when entering someone else's litter box.

Never stop exploring, unless the trip is going to interrupt nap time.

Those who are willing
to unroll the yarn ball
of life are more likely
to be happy!

Never trust a friend wearing a top hat, no matter how cute they look.

Always be willing to lend
a helping hand.

Sing louder when those around you say you can't sing.

Always take time to relax and enjoy the world around you.

Be adaptable
when necessary.
If you fit, sit!

Don't believe everything you see online.

Every mind is born
with the spirit of curiosity.
Never stop exploring.

Reading a good book will take you far away from your everyday worries.

It's important to maintain a well-groomed appearance. You never know when you'll need to impress.

Always move quietly when in sneak mode. Make sure they never see you coming!

Adventure begins by getting off the ground and seeing the world from a different perspective.

Soak up as much
sun as you can!

Wrinkles are proof that you're living life to the fullest.

Whether fur or feather, we can all live together!

High-fives are good
for morale!

It's okay to have your guard up—just know that it's okay to trust sometimes, too.

It's never to late to
learn new tricks!

Every second is a gift—that's why they call it the present!

Be grateful for all that
life gives you.

Be careful when you start pulling string, you never know what may be on the other end.

Best friends
are furr-ever.

Live every day like it's
your birthday.

Appreciate the little things in life.

Be the queen of your castle.

Images from Shutterstock.com: Linn Currie (Cover, 15); Rita_Kochmarjova (3); eurobanks (5); MartynaPixie (7); Lightspruch (9); U__Photo (11); glenda (13); Esin Deniz (17); Alones (19); vvvita (21, 29); New Africa (23, 39); Tik.Tanased (25); ShineTerra (27); AltamashUrooj (31); Viacheslav Lopatin (33); Giga25 (35); KOSKA ill (37); Bachkova Natalia (40-41); Nils Jacobi (43); Masarik (44-45); Creative Cat Studio (47); createthis (49); Luxurious Ragdoll (51); SerPhoto (52-53); ANURAK PONGPATIMET (55); beton studio (57); Chendongshan (59); Antonov Serg (61); GoodFocused (63).

ISBN 978-1-4971-0559-1

Library of Congress Control Number: 2024925893

To learn more about the other great books from Fox Chapel Publishing, or to find a retailer near you, call toll-free 800-457-9112, or visit us at www.FoxChapelPublishing.com.

You can also send mail to:
903 Square Street
Mount Joy, PA 17552.

We are always looking for talented authors. To submit an idea, please send a brief inquiry to acquisitions@foxchapelpublishing.com.

Printed in China

First printing